one hit wonders

one hit Wonders

CHRIS WELCH
Photography by
DUNCAN SOAR

NEW HOLLAND

CONTENTS

INTRODUCTION

'I was famous overnight – but it all disappeared just as quickly.' The poignant cry of singer Tracie Young evokes all the joy, delight and heartbreak experienced by that remarkable breed, the one hit wonder. When 18-year-old Tracie hit the Top 10 with 'The House That Jack Built' in 1983, a bright showbiz career beckoned. But she saw fame fade as her public moved on, eager for new faces and fresh sounds. Tracie's mixed blessings will be familiar to many of the artists whose remarkable stories are told in this fascinating book.

'What becomes of the broken hearted?' Jimmy Ruffin posed the question with his 1966 smash. At least he was rewarded with three more chart busters. For many an aspiring singer, band or composer, the one-off hit can be a painful affair. A really *big* record can transform lives in uplifting, positive ways. New careers, exciting opportunities, even in rare cases, rich rewards and a rock'n'roll pension can follow. And if the hope of finding a follow-up becomes an elusive phantom, there is always solace in the sense of achievement. Many of our one hit wonders will say defiantly to their critics: 'Well, at least I had one more hit than *you*!'

The Entries
The criterion for inclusion is simple. Contenders have to be British with one major Top 30 hit during their career. Naturally, most bands and artists try to gain a follow-up. If their subsequent singles only crept into the Top 40, then it is the Top 30 BIGGIE that remains forever embedded in the public's memory. Think of the song and you immediately think of the band or artist and vice versa.

Opposite: Sheer bliss – thumbing through the racks of 45s in her local record store, a teenage pop picker finds that elusive hit single. 'Can I have Connie Francis' latest?' 'Yes, that'll be five shillings and sixpence dear.'

"LAST NIGHT I DREAMED"
WINIFRED
ATWELL
"Lipstick on your Collar"
CONNIE FRANCIS
M-G-M
M-G-M
TODAYS
TOP TEN
RECORDS
LONDON

We even considered including those giants of heavy rock Led Zeppelin. Although the band fought shy of releasing singles during the 70s, some of their songs were so commercial that their US record company defied management policy and put them out anyway. As a result the group had six Top 40 hits in America including 'Whole Lotta Love', which got to No 4 in Billboard as early as December 1969. The band had always said 'no' to UK singles but in 1997, nearly two decades after the original group had broken up, 'Whole Lotta Love' finally entered the UK singles charts and peaked at No 21. The pulsating riff tune had long been familiar as the theme to *Top Of The Pops*. Yet the band's most famous song, their extended ballad 'Stairway to Heaven' from the 1971 *Led Zeppelin IV* album was never released as a single. Technically, Led Zeppelin could be hailed as one hit wonders in the UK. But somehow, it's not a role that seems appropriate.

The Golden Years of Pop

As we survey four decades of hit making, we can see that the 60s was the age of 'groups of guitars', as Decca A&R man Dick Rowe famously described them. The 70s saw glam rockers battling with ballad singers and novelty acts. The 80s brought New Wave and techno while the more serious 90s was dominated by Indie and dance music. It was also the era of the 'bedroom genius' making hits with minimal equipment and defying music industry logic. Whatever their chosen style throughout the decades, one hit wonders remain a crucial factor in the charts, bringing surprise and delight to the fans; fury and indignation to the critics.

Whatever the artistic merits of those fondly remembered hits – and they range from the sublime to the outrageous – they show pop democracy in action. Sensitive songwriters with a political conscience, brilliant prog rockers, or just wannabes with a guitar and a song? Everyone could have a go at having a hit.

Opposite: 'How's about that then?' DJ Jimmy Saville introducing the first edition of BBC chart show Top Of The Pops *in 1964.* TOTP *celebrated its 2000th edition in September 2002.*

Right: 'Greetings pop pickers!' DJ Alan 'Fluff' Freeman had a supply of catch phrases when hosting his popular BBC radio show Pick Of The Pops *launched in 1961. 'Alright? Not 'alf.'*

9

John Otway was one artist who certainly had a go when he and Wild Willy Barrett released seminal punk anthem 'Really Free' in 1977. The pair's single spent eight weeks in the charts and everyone remembers it as a classic one hit wonder. Yet it only reached No 27 at its highest point. John enjoyed an even bigger hit in the year 2002, when his latest single 'Bunsen Burner' soared to No 9 in the charts. It was just in time to help celebrate his 50th birthday. However, as the latter was a hit in the new, rather than old Millennium, it has been decreed that 'Really Free' is the most appropriate contender for Mr Otway's one hit wonder status. Apart from that, it's a really great record and John's renewed success shows that not only 90s artist are destined to strike lucky again.

Hedgehoppers Anonymous remained anonymous throughout their short hop through the charts with 1965 No 5 hit 'It's Good News Week'. It was penned by 'pop mogul' Jonathan King, who claimed the band were all former RAF chaps.

Some argue that pop is more about market forces than merit. But the big question is: 'Does the record make you want to whistle or dance?' If the answer is 'yes' then staff will be working overtime at the nation's record counters, while the eager artists pray their song will be No 1. There's no doubting the importance of radio and club DJs, whose personal play lists can strongly influence the record buying public. In many cases it has been the enthusiasm of top jocks that has helped otherwise unknown newcomers to the top of the charts. Yet, despite all the promotion in the world, there has been a significant fall in the numbers of singles purchased since the 60s, 70s and early 80s. Then, many more thousands of copies needed to be sold to gain a high chart position, unlike today, when a band or artist can make an impact with much lower sales.

That Special Something

What strange alchemy transmutes one record into pure gold, while others flop? Strangely enough, artists always seem to know when they've pulled it off. They emerge bleary-eyed from the studio looking unnervingly confident. 'We weren't surprised' is one relaxed reaction. 'We knew the record was special.' Yet there is often a fight to get a great song past a disbelieving manager or sceptical A&R man. The determined artist then turns to the DJs who they know can pick a winner. Many a one hit wonder has pressed up and mailed out his or her own records in the hope of convincing the world it should learn to sing their song.

Fred Wedlock, that most unlikely chart star, and folk singer from the West Country was stunned when his offering, 'The Oldest Swinger In Town', became a national favourite in 1980. Fred says it

Neil Reid signs the sleeve of his one-off hit single 'Mother Of Mine' in Chappell's, while his fans look on in admiration. The song got to No 2 in 1972 and spent 20 weeks in the charts.

was all thanks to Radio 1 DJ Noel Edmonds. 'He played the song twice during the same Sunday morning show. Noel said: "This is fantastic, it's gonna be a hit." Then my phone started ringing and it didn't stop for months. Everything went mad.'

And madness is never far behind when pop stardom beckons. Jyoti Mishra found his world turned upside down when he created an ingenious No 1 as White Town with 'Your Woman' in 1997. Says Jyoti: 'It became the most requested record on Radio 1 and when Virgin Radio played it as well I became a news story. "Bloke in bedroom makes record." I had more requests than Oasis and I was quite freaked out.'

Despite the upheaval caused by overnight fame, Jyoti is glad that people at least recognise his musical skills. In our relentless quest to track down the 'Wonders', some proved less keen to be reminded of their one-off hit. A well-known progressive rock band felt that a solitary hit didn't really represent their oeuvre. And a singer whose career flowered briefly in the 90s was adamant he was no fly-by-night. Indeed, the 90s have proved less fruitful in terms of one hit wonders, mainly because its youthful protagonists are convinced they are due for another hit – and very soon.

¹² But those in their 60s, who were stars in the 60s, are clearly delighted to be reminded of past glories. They appreciate the interest and are only too happy to remember the beneficial impact on their lives. For them a hit was a defining moment. They felt rewarded for their past commitment. One hit or no hit? They know which is better.

Typically Tropical are proud one hit wonders. When they topped the charts in 1975 with 'Barbados', it was their first record. They never had another hit themselves, but when their song was later covered by The Venga Boys, it was No 1 again, proving the timeless appeal of a catchy tune.

When Ralph McTell unveiled his wonderful 'Streets Of London' in 1974 it was already a hit with loyal fans and remains indelibly associated with its composer. Ralph tells how the true meaning of the song remains as relevant today, as when it first brought him a taste of stardom.

Some songs seem to have mysterious properties and are destined to dominate the lives of all who dare evoke them. 'Spirit In The Sky' was a No 1 for its American composer Norman Greenbaum in 1970. The same marvellously atmospheric tune, with its weirdly psychedelic effects, was back at No 1 in 1986, this time by Britain's cheerful Doctor And The Medics. When it was revived yet again in spring 2003, by former *Pop Idol* contestant Gareth Gates and comedy team The Kumars, their hit video dominated TV pop channels for weeks.

Stealing the Show
A common thread through all these stories is the all-important appearance on BBC TV's chart show *Top Of The Pops*. It was especially satisfying that The Mock Turtles appeared on the show

'Cor baby, that's really gold!' John Otway hugs the gold disc that says 'You are a one hit wonder'. Or in his case – a TWO hit wonder.

the very week they were contributing to this book. Amidst a busy schedule of interviews and photograph sessions the band, led by singer and guitarist Martin Coogan, raced to Television Centre to perform 'Can You Dig It?'. Their catchy tune had peaked at No 18 back in March 1991, but thanks to a Vodafone TV ad campaign that revitalised the riff (originally dashed off by Mr Coogan as a B side) it was back in the charts again in March 2003. 'We're now "dual hit wonders" – quite a rarity!' says Martin.

While *Top Of The Pops* has celebrated the hits, other TV shows have provided the showcase that brought new names to the public's attention. Certainly artists like Tammy Jones were grateful for the exposure on Hughie Green's famed talent show *Opportunity Knocks* and BBC TV's *The Old Grey Whistle Test* hosted by Bob Harris gave a boost to John Otway and many other musical 'outsiders' and underground acts.

The Here and Now

The comic irony of transient stardom appeals to comedian Graham Fellows. The satirist was delighted when his creation Jilted John captivated fans in 1977 at the height of punk rock. Today Graham is John Shuttleworth the Sheffield keyboard virtuoso, who finds his former character Jilted John too much of a teenage rebel to recreate in his current stage show. As Mr Shuttleworth says, with quiet satisfaction: '"Jilted John" was always meant to be a one hit wonder.'

It's doubtful if Max Splodge of Splodgenessabounds had any such master plan when he created the highly ridiculous 'Two Pints Of Lager And A Packet Of Crisps Please'. This miniscule protest song of the unfulfilled lager drinker stunned the record industry and indeed Max and all his mates, when it got to No 7 in the UK charts in 1980. Who'd heard anything as silly as this less-than-B-side of a hit? Yet Max ensured his plaintive cry became a national catchphrase to match 'Gordon is a

Opposite: Singer Clive Jackson dispenses good medicine with his band Doctor And The Medics. Still touring and entertaining fans, the Medics invoke the 'Spirit In The Sky' – a hit for them in 1986.

Steve Elson, former singer with Broken English, seen in his latter-day role as maraca shaking 'Nick Dagger' of the Counterfeit Stones.

moron'. Could anyone survive such a hit? Max certainly has and is now touring the world on a regular basis – thank you!

Many of our former chart toppers remain committed to the business of recording, and are able to carry on thanks to the dot.com revolution. So, even if record companies drop them, they can always turn to the Internet, where home produced CDs can be marketed and sold. Others have found fresh ways to utilise their energy. Effervescent Tracie Young is now a radio DJ, who resolutely tries to avoid playing her own records. Hailed as a 'cultural icon' by one young novelist, she became the toast of pop nostalgia addicts after a guest appearance on BBC TV's *Never Mind the Buzzcocks*.

Some former teenage tunesmiths are now engaged in grown up business, working as financial advisers, pilots, commercial artists, teachers or actors. Others have less glamorous day jobs but retain their love of music, reviving their original bands and seeking out audiences, even if they're only in their local pub.

Only a small minority seem damaged by chartdom. There are rumours that one former musician has been seen roaming the streets, claiming he has been abducted by aliens. Most are well adjusted to their role and are perfectly happy, like Tammy Jones who had a hit with 'Let Me Try Again' in 1975. She now lives in New Zealand, where she cheerfully stages a 'Fish, Chips And Knees Up Mother Brown' cabaret for tourists.

Dave Lee Travis helped many a one hit wonder to stardom by playing their records on radio and TV. Here he hosts Top Of The Pops.

Certainly none seem to regret that opportunity knocked only once. One hit wonders feel only pleasure at the memory of those extraordinary days when charts ruled their lives; when fans cheered and studio lights glared as their TV hosts shouted 'Welcome to *Top Of The Pops*!'

CHRIS WELCH

THE ADVERTS

'Gary Gilmore's Eyes' No 18, September 1977
Line up: Tim 'TV' Smith (vocals, guitar), Gaye Advert (vocals, bass), Howard Pickup (guitar), Laurie Driver (drums)

TIM 'TV' SMITH: Gaye Advert and I met at Torquay Art College. We moved up to London in the summer of 1976 and started playing at the Roxy. It was during the early stages of punk and our inspiration came from Iggy Pop and The New York Dolls.We weren't intent on being brilliant musicians; we just wanted to get our ideas across and punk gave us that freedom. We started rehearsing with Howard, then later with Laurie. Brian James of The Damned introduced the band to Stiff Records and within weeks we'd cut our first single 'One Chord Wonders', which was also one of the names we had for the band. However, it had too much of a one hit wonder connotation, so we ditched it for The Adverts. Our second single, 'Gary Gilmore's Eyes', was about the eyes of an American murderer that were transplanted in to another man. We had great reviews, so it wasn't a surprise when it was a hit. Appearing on *Top Of The Pops* was great publicity but rather a tacky experience. Punk musicians were treated like cattle, and we weren't an exception. I was reprimanded for not singing when they gave me an aluminium microphone; and they wouldn't let me wear a chain because it could be misconstrued

as 'an offensive weapon'. In 1979 we released our second album *Cast Of Thousands*. It was a commercial disaster and the critics had a field-day. The bad reviews proved too much. We changed drummers, the guitarist left and it was never the same.

Gaye stopped playing the day the band broke up and she has never picked up a bass guitar again. She now works for Social Services as a home help team manager. Laurie Driver moved to Iceland and, sadly, Howard Pickup died from a brain tumour a few years ago. I carried on working with bands such as The Explorers, and since 1991 I've released five albums as a solo artist, including 'Generation Y'. There is still an audience for live music.

'"Gary Gilmore's Eyes" was about the eyes of an American murderer.'

ANEKA

'Japanese Boy' No 1, August 1981

ANEKA (MARY SANDEMAN): I had no aspirations to be a pop singer; it just happened. My musical background was in Gaelic folk music and not in pop. However, I had rearranged some of my pieces into a contemporary style for an album, hoping that young people might become more interested in Gaelic music. 'Japanese Boy' was written by my arranger Bobby Heatlie. I asked him if he wrote songs himself and, if so, would he write one for me? He eventually came up with 'Japanese Boy', which was a huge hit. The record company said that they couldn't use my real name – Mary Sandeman – because it just wasn't marketable. So we found 'Aneka' in the Edinburgh phone book. I learned that 'Japanese Boy' was No 1 while I was singing a programme of Scots and Gaelic music at the Edinburgh Festival. Oddly, I never went to Japan. They thought it sounded 'too Chinese', which was strange. There was an attempt at a follow up called 'Little Lady', but where do you go after you've had a hit with a distinctive song, wearing a Japanese kimono and a black wig? You have to change your image and it really didn't work. I suppose it all lasted about two years. During that time I was still working with the

Scottish Fiddle Orchestra and singing Scots songs at Burns Nights and St Andrew's Nights all over the world.

People still know me as Aneka, although I have a grown-up family with two sons. I've stopped singing in public now, but I've started having singing lessons again and have a new CD planned. I'm also taking a journey down a different route by studying the art of using the voice for healing. It's called the 'Mozart' effect and I find it quite intriguing. It's to do with finding myself and helping others through using the voice. I've reached that stage where family and friends mean the most in life. I had a ball when I was No 1 and have no regrets at all. It was such fun.

'I had no aspirations to be a pop singer; it just happened.'

THE BRAT

'Chalk Dust: The Umpire Strikes Back' No 19, July 1982
Line up: Kaplan Kaye and Roger Kitter (vocals and commentary)

KAPLAN KAYE: Roger and I made 'Chalk Dust' as a spoof of John McEnroe when he was Wimbledon tennis champion. As a youngster I had aspirations of becoming a pop star. Instead I became an actor and appeared in radio's 'Mrs Dale's Diary' and played 'Henry' in BBC TV's *Just William*. I toured the northern night clubs but didn't enjoy it. I was singing in Wakefield one night when a guy came up on stage, ripped the guitar off me and kicked in my amplifier. I thought 'I'm not doing this anymore'. So I stayed behind the scenes and worked for Dick James Music as a sound engineer. My best mate was Roger Kitter the comedian. He'd been doing 'Who Do You Do?' the impressions show, and we decided to do a comedy record. We mulled over a few ideas and thought of doing a McEnroe spoof. We recorded it with Pete Wingfield on keyboards and Ray Russell on guitar. Roger played McEnroe, I was the umpire and it was put out as The Brat. We made three appearances on *Top Of The Pops* with Roger in a headband and me sitting in an umpire's chair. McEnroe hated it! It was the year

when McEnroe was headlining the news with his tantrums and he said we were jumping on the bandwagon, which was quite true! He wasn't impressed when we sneaked into his press party in a Kensington hotel. Roger went to the loo, quickly got changed and came out in his McEnroe headband. He stormed the photo shoot and started singing 'You cannot be serious!' while I shouted 'The ball was OUT!' It was hysterical. We got so much press coverage the record took off and reached No 19 in July 1982. It stayed in the charts for eight weeks and was even No 1 in Belgium. We didn't make a follow up. I now run Kaplan Kaye Enterprises, a theatrical agency, management, music publishing and recording company. Roger Kitter tours with Jim Davidson doing stand-up comedy and he also has a leading role in the new film *Suzie Gold*.

'McEnroe hated it!'

BRIAN AND MICHAEL

'Matchstalk Men And Matchstalk Cats And Dogs' No 1, April 1978
Line up: Michael Coleman (lead vocal), Brian Burke (backing vocals, guitar), St Winifred's Choir (backing vocals), Tintwistle Brass Band, Kevin Parrott (Producer)

KEVIN PARROTT: Mick and I were in a soul band in the 60s called the Big Sound. Mick is a great soul singer, although 'Matchstalk Men' is a folksy middle of the road-ish song. When the band split, I joined Manchester rock band Oscar. Mick and I had stayed friends, and he began writing songs, one being 'Matchstalk', inspired by northern artist LS Lowry. Mick had been brought up where Lowry had painted. I borrowed the money to produce the record, and wanted to paint a Lowry picture in sound. We used St Winifred's choir and my local brass band. It was tough to get a deal, however, luckily we had a call to appear on BBC TV's *Swap Shop* and secured a contract with Pye Records on the same day. A week after the single was released, Brian Burke bowed out, and I decided to leave Oscar and live the 'life of Brian'. DJ Peter Powell and his producer Ted Beston championed the record every Sunday morning on Radio 1. It made the charts at 45, but was pulled as it was wrongly suspected of being hyped due to the bias of northern sales. We made seven appearances on *Top Of The Pops* and, because of its wide family appeal, we made it to No 1. We never expected such a big hit; it was probably the second biggest British single of the year after the Bee Gees' 'Night Fever', which was the highest seller. Mick won the coveted Ivor Novello Award for the best lyric of the year.

Since then Mick has written a Lowry musical containing outstanding songs and, in recent years, has continued to work successfully as a solo performer. I have been fortunate enough to carve out a lucrative career in advertising. We started performing together again in 2002, and we are incredibly moved by the reception we get. We did a reunion concert at Manchester's Lowry Centre with the original St Winnie's girls who are now in their 30s. It was great fun!

'It was the second biggest British single of the year.'

BROKEN ENGLISH

'Comin' On Strong' No 18, May 1987
Line up: Steve Elson (vocals), Alan Coates (guitar), Jamie Moses (guitar), Steve Stroud (bass), Howard Tibble (drums)

STEVE ELSON: In 1983 I was living in Hertfordshire and had a recording studio at the top of my house. I was messing around with a Rolling Stones tribute band called the Strolling Bones that guitarist Tom Nolan and I had started. We played at parties and I thought it would be a laugh to make a Stones-sounding record. I put a demo together and took it to Oliver Smallman, a song plugger. He said it was too good to waste and suggested I form a new band around the record. I rang up some old guitarist friends, including Alan Coates and Jamie Moses. We added a drummer and bassist to replace my drum machine track. A lot of people thought we chose Broken English because of Marianne Faithfull's 1979 album but, in fact, I got the name out of a dictionary. EMI sent the single out as 'white label' copies, saying we were a new, mystery band. People thought it was by the Stones and it was played to death on radio. Then we explained we were Broken English. On the record we had a ranting, shouting introduction and lots of overdubbed guitars. I wrote the song on the labels of 12 bottles of Pils

that I'd drunk at a Sunday lunchtime session after a row with my girlfriend. I plugged in my guitar and the riff came from pure anger. That's how the phrase 'She's comin' on strong!' started. We made a video and the song became a Top 20 hit. On the strength of this success we recorded an album, but it wasn't released until after our next single flopped. The guy who signed us left the company and his replacement didn't like Stones-style bands. I couldn't hold the thing together and Broken English drifted apart in 1989. Ever since, I've been lead singer with the Counterfeit Stones – the ultimate Stones tribute band!

'I wrote the song on the labels of 12 bottles of Pils.'

CLIMAX BLUES BAND

'Couldn't Get It Right' No 10, October 1976
*Line up: Colin Cooper (vocals, sax), Peter Haycock (guitar, vocals), Derek Holt (bass), Richard Jones
(keyboards) and John Cuffley (drums)*

COLIN COOPER: We started out as a pure blues band in Stafford in the 60s. I had played at a Stoke-on-Trent
club called The Place which featured blues legends like John Lee Hooker and Howling Wolf. We were on our ninth
album, believe it or not, when we had a hit with 'Couldn't Get It Right'. We'd always released radio-friendly tracks
to promote albums but by 1976 we needed a commercial pop single. After we finished recording, our new
producer Mike Vernon laughingly related how he had told Peter Green of Fleetwood Mac that 'Albatross' would
never be a success. In 1973 the song had reached No 2 in the UK. We thought, 'Oh my God – and we were
expecting him to spot a hit for us.' Our manager Miles Copeland didn't think there was a track on the finished
album that was a potential hit, and he tried to persuade us to do an Elvis Presley cover. Instead, we put together
'Couldn't Get It Right', which proved to be unbelievably catchy. I wrote the lyrics and sang it, and the song
became the first record we'd produced ourselves. Miles agreed it was special. In 1976 it was a hit in England,
and the following year it rocketed up the charts in America where it got to No 3. It was played on the radio around

the clock. But the aftermath was rather strange. We changed management and record company, a move that

was handled badly. In the quest for follow-up hits we kind of lost the
plot, and the band began to change personnel in 1977. Climax Blues
now includes myself, Lester Hunt (guitar), George Glover (keyboards),
Neil Simpson (bass) and Roy Adams (drums). We've gone back to the
roots and our latest album *Big Blues* consists of classic Willie Dixon
tunes like 'Little Red Rooster'. When you reach my age, playing the
pop star would be a bit undignified. But we still play 'Couldn't Get It
Right' and it still sounds great.

**'It was played on the radio around
the clock.'**

DOCTOR AND THE MEDICS

'Spirit In The Sky' No 1, May 1986
Line up: Clive Jackson (vocals), Steve McGuire (guitar), Richard Searle (bass), Steven Ritchie (drums) and the Anadin Brothers (backing vocals)

CLIVE JACKSON: I formed an embryonic version of Doctor And The Medics in 1982 when I was a DJ and starting the psychedelic revival. I ran clubs called The Clinic and Alice In Wonderland. The band built up a massive 'live' following before we signed to the IRS label and had a hit. We used to do a lot of covers, including Norman Greenbaum's 1970 song 'Spirit In The Sky'. I had a bizarre dream in which I bumped into John and Yoko, and John said, 'Marc Bolan is playing in a pub over the road'. We went over and Marc was strumming acoustic guitar and singing 'Spirit In The Sky'. Funnily enough that was the last time I had a pint with Marc Bolan and John Lennon! I told the band about my dream and that's why our version tips its hat to T Rex, with Tony Visconti-style strings. We shot a video for £2500 in a church hall featuring swirling patterns made from cut-out card. It was shown on TV's *Saturday Superstore* and as a result shot to No 1. It sold 2.3 million copies and was No 1 in 18

countries. I had a conversation on the radio with Norman Greenbaum and he didn't sound too chuffed. He had been managing a hamburger bar and got the sack because of all these phone calls asking how he felt about the song being a hit again. His bosses said, 'If you're such a big star, you don't need to be working here.' But we had a lot of fun and partied all around the world. After our second album, we broke up. I tell people I'm a multi-millionaire but we didn't make much money. Steve McGuire went on to work as production manager for Badly Drawn Boy, and four years ago I put a new version of the band together. We do 100 shows a year. Until Gareth Gates had a hit with 'Spirit' everyone said that it was the only record to have been No 1 by two one hit wonders – ourselves and Norman Greenbaum. I've heard Gareth now wants to be a serious R&B artist. So 'Spirit In The Sky' might have been his last No 1 as well!

'Our version tips its hat to T Rex.'

EDDIE AND THE HOT RODS

'Do Anything You Wanna Do' No 9, August 1977
Line up: Barrie Masters (vocals), Dave Higgs (guitar), Graeme Douglas (guitars), Paul Gray (bass), and Steve Nicol (drums)

BARRIE MASTERS: I suppose the Hot Rods were like the acceptable faces of punk. We used to pack out the Marquee in London with our high-energy shows. We had three singles out before 'Do Anything You Wanna Do' was a Top Ten hit. Dave Higgs, our guitar player, had written most of our first album and then Graeme Douglas joined the band from the Kursaal Flyers. Graeme and Ed Hollis, our manager, began writing together and they came up with the hit, which was in a slightly different vein from what we had been doing. Straight away we knew it had potential. Steve Lillywhite did a great job as producer. It got to No 9 in the UK and went higher in other countries. It sold slowly at first and then began picking up after three appearances on *Top Of The Pops*. The song was a hit all over the summer and stayed in the charts for weeks. It was a fantastic feeling and chart success also doubled our audience at gigs. I remember we appeared on Marc Bolan's TV show the week before he died.

His death was a real shame. In those days every record label had its own punk band. CBS had the Clash, and Polydor had the Jam. Island were always good to us and we should never have moved, but we were talked into going to EMI. They were great at first, but after we did an album called *Fish'N'Chips* in 1980, they just let it slip out and the album went nowhere. We never made any money. It all came in and went out very fast. At least we had a lot of fun and the audiences were great. The band hung on until 1981, then split up. I've reformed the Hot Rods since then for gigs, but I don't earn enough to stay professional. I now work as a driver for a glass company that carries out a lot of work for the police, doing emergency boarding up. If I give the company lots of notice, I can go off and do a new album or tour with the band, so I'm very lucky.

'We appeared on Marc Bolan's TV show a week before he died.'

EDISON LIGHTHOUSE

'Love Grows (Where My Rosemary Goes)' No 1, January 1970
Line up: Tony Burrows (lead vocals), Stuart Edwards (lead guitar and vocals), Ray Dorey (guitar, lead vocals), Dave Taylor (bass) and George Weyman (drums)

STUART EDWARDS: When the Edison Lighthouse thing happened we were a semi-pro 'covers' band from Windsor called Greenfield Hammer. In December 1969 our agent told us a couple of songwriters, Tony McCauley and Barry Mason, were holding auditions in London. Only two other bands turned up. We weren't particularly good but the others were useless. The writers wanted us to back their in-house vocalist, Tony Burrows, on a song called 'Love Grows'. Tony also sang with Brotherhood Of Man, The Pipkins and White Plains, and he once appeared with all four bands on the same edition of *Top Of The Pops*. 'Love Grows' was our first single and our one and only hit. It was No 1 in the UK, No 5 in the States and No 4 in Japan. However, Tony didn't want to tour with the band, which was a problem. He had too many other interests and was quite shrewd, unlike us lads. The hit happened so quickly it caught us all by surprise. We toured the big clubs where audiences expected a cabaret act. Instead, they got five scruffy lads doing Steppenwolf covers. The money was good but at some gigs we died quite a death. We tried to get a follow-up but we couldn't manage it, and in 1971 we split up.

I worked in the film industry as a sound engineer, then retired and moved with my family to Cornwall. Tony Burrows is a brilliant, natural singer, but he is pretty much retired too. Ray Dorey is a successful businessman and we can't tempt him out of retirement. Sadly, our drummer George Weyman died some 20 years ago. However, when Dave Taylor moved to Cornwall, he suggested I get out my old guitar. Dave now works for Modern Organic Products, but he loves to play, so we formed a duo version of Edison Lighthouse in 2002 and it's been absolutely fantastic. We play 'Love Grows' every night and say 'This is a medley of our hit!'

'They got five scruffy lads doing Steppenwolf covers.'

KAREL FIALKA

'Hey Matthew' No 9, September 1987

KAREL FIALKA: My son Matthew was aged six when we made 'Hey Matthew'. I taped his answers to questions about what he watched on TV, often violent images, and used a sampler to get the background effects. I'd been around bands since the 60s. I went to Spain in the 70s and came back to find myself in the midst of the burgeoning punk revolution. Prior to punk it felt as if you needed a PhD in music before you could pick up a guitar. Now you were able to go back to your roots, strum three chords and still have something to say. Synthesizers were also making an impact, and I loved them and their possibilities. I recorded a song called 'Arm Band', which was rejected by various record companies. But I was bigheaded enough to think it was pretty good, so I had 1,000 copies pressed and sent them out to DJs. As a result I was signed to Charlie Gillett's Oval label, and in 1980 I had a radio hit with 'The Eyes Have It', which got to No 52 in the UK charts. Eventually, I released 'Hey Matthew', which had been around for a few years by then, on Miles Copeland's IRS label. When it was a hit I wasn't surprised. In fact, I felt it could have been a No 1. Matthew himself didn't appear with me on *Top Of The Pops* as he was too young. Instead, we got an agency in France to find lads of Matthew's age to take his place, and each TV appearance saw a new 'Matthew' standing by my side. Once they brought along two boys who both wanted to be on the show. 'You choose', they said. I couldn't decide between them, so I ended up with two 'Matthews'.

The real Matthew is now at college. In the song he says he wants to be a train driver or a pirate. At the moment he's a mountain biker with a broken arm. As for me, I'm currently recording three albums, I have my own studio and am occasionally a music lecturer in the Highlands of Scotland. Would I like another hit record? For sure!

'I couldn't decide, so I ended up with two Matthews.'

FIDDLER'S DRAM

'Day Trip To Bangor' No 4, December 1979
Line up: Cathy Lesurf (vocals, bodhran, bells), Chris Taylor (banjo, guitar, mouth organ, bouzouki, dulcimer), Alan Prosser (guitar, bass, bones, dulcimer), Ian Telfer (fiddle, psaltery, English concertina), Ian Kearey (bass)

CHRIS TAYLOR: Before the hit, we had been trying to scrape a living playing in folk clubs. We formed the group in 1976 and Fiddler's Dram was named after an American tune called 'Give The Fiddler A Dram', which originally came from Scotland. We got a record deal and recorded an album produced by Roger Holt. An acoustic version of 'Day Trip To Bangor', a song about a Lancashire mill workers' charabanc outing – 'all for under a pound', was on the album. 'Bangor' was written by Debbie Cook, who went on to write scripts for *The Archers* and *EastEnders*. Roger Holt felt it would make a good novelty song, so we said, 'Why not?' We got in a drummer and electric bass player to pop it up and released a remixed version in November 1979. Curiously enough it started hitting the charts and got to No 4 by Christmas, when Pink Floyd was No 1 with 'Another Brick In The Wall'. It was a very strange and freakish occurrence. When we did *Top Of The Pops,* I can recall each member of Boney M turning up in their own white stretch limo. There was a flurry of activity after the hit and we played at big venues throughout the country. But the novelty soon wore off. As Fiddler's Dram faded out, we returned to playing with the Oyster Band, which was our main group. I made about £8,000 from the hit, but I can't say I spent it wisely. I was going through a divorce and had to pay off my ex-wife. I also drank a lot of it away.

I stayed in the Oyster Band until 1984 and now teach music at Canterbury College. Alan Prosser and Ian Telfer are still with the Oyster Band. Cathy Lesurf went on to sing with the Albion Band and Fairport Convention. She now lives in Nottingham and still does occasional gigs. Ian Kearey is married with children and works as an editor and writer.

'It was a very strange and freakish occurrence.'

FLYING LIZARDS

'Money (That's What I Want)' No 4, August 1979
Line up: Deborah Evans-Stickland (vocals), David Cunningham (guitar, piano, producer)

DEBORAH EVANS-STICKLAND: I first met David Cunningham in the painting department at Maidstone Art College. For some reason he thought I would probably sing like Tina Turner, which I didn't. There wasn't any great plan when the Flying Lizards was put together, except that David liked Phil Spector and wanted to be a producer. We recorded 'Money' in a freezing cold meat fridge in Brixton. It was very low-budget and only cost £6.50 to make. Was I excited when it was a hit? No. Not really. We didn't tour as the Flying Lizards as I was just a recording artist, but I do remember doing a gig in a warehouse in Europe. It was madness. I had to tell David to turn on the microphone – that's all I remember. When 'Money' went to No 4, we started getting a lot of public attention. There's nothing wrong with exhibitionism, but it can stir up envy and that's what I disliked about having a hit record. The envy meant that any camaraderie between me and David quickly went out of the window. There was an album by the Flying Lizards which was a Top 10 flop, but my vocals were wiped off. Instead an actress was brought in and she mimicked my voice, but I don't know if that worked. Maybe in the history of the Flying Lizards that's why we became one hit wonders.

In 1985 I started training to become a psychotherapist and qualified in 1989. Then I had my child, a boy who is now aged 13. I returned to work ten years ago, helping people with learning disabilities. David now has a recording studio and produces film music. I'm still singing and have recorded a blues album. I've done a very menacing version of Jimi Hendrix's 'Hey Joe', and have also recorded 'Walk On By' for an album by Richard X.

'Was I excited when it was a hit? No. Not really.'

HONEYBUS

'I Can't Let Maggie Go' No 8, March 1968
Line up: Pete Dello (vocals, guitar), Colin Hart (guitar, vocals), Ray Cane (bass) and Pete Kircher (drums)

PETE DELLO: I met Ray Cane when he was playing with The Outlaws and we began writing songs together. The name 'Honeybus' came about when I said I wanted something warm like honey. A bus drove past and Ray said 'How about Honeybus?' In 1966 I suffered a collapsed lung and while I was in hospital, I decided I didn't want to tour anymore. However, our record company were expecting a four-piece band. We put out feelers and found Pete Kircher who sang and played drums, and Colin Hart who also had a fantastic voice. By the time of our second single I'd learnt how to arrange music, and after hearing a woodwind piece by Mozart, I decided to experiment with classical instruments. I blended two oboes, a cor anglais and bassoon, and the result was 'I Can't Let Maggie Go'. It was a huge hit. Maggie Thatcher used it as her crowd warm-up and a different version was featured in a Nimble Bread advert. Although 'Maggie' was a success, somehow we got into a pickle. The band wanted to tour, but I wanted to stay in the studio. It all got too much for me, and I left in 1969. The split was amicable and I've never regretted it. Once I had gone Ray and Colin came into their own as a songwriters. Sadly, though, they didn't get any more hits and broke up.

Pete is now in the sign writing business. Pete has given up drumming, but Colin still does a one-man band show. Ray Cane moved to Australia and is a financial adviser. I teach guitar and piano and write mainly classical music. Last year I went to Spain to perform with Colin which was fun. There's still loads of interest in Honeybus. The 60s were when musicians last ran the show – we were the true experimenters!

'Maggie Thatcher used it as her crowd warm-up.'

JILTED JOHN

'Jilted John' No 4, August 1978

GRAHAM FELLOWS: Jilted John started life when I was at drama school in Manchester in 1977. There was a guitar lying around in the canteen and someone showed me how to play a chord. From then on there was no stopping me. I had intended to become a serious actor, but I'm glad I didn't since my career has been much more interesting because of the music. 'Jilted John' was always meant to be a one hit wonder. It was a parody of punk. Love song lyrics never rang true, but John Otway's 'Really Free' did and it was a big influence on my work. Everyone knows the song as 'Gordon Is A Moron', but we were trying to be arty and minimalist, so it became 'Jilted John'. I made a demo of it in a local studio with a friend, Bernard Kelly, who played Gordon and who later did the hand jive on *Top Of The Pops*. I took the tape to Rabid Records and they asked me to re-record it with legendary producer Martin Hannett. John Peel started playing it, and I got my sister to write in and request it, which is highly illegal, isn't it? When it got into the charts I was at a Christian Youth camp. I wasn't a Christian but it was full of gorgeous girls from the Home Counties. I mysteriously disappeared during the holiday when I was whisked off to appear on *Top Of The Pops*. Everyone thought I'd been to a funeral. My only regret

was being too sensible – I bought a house with the money, when perhaps I should have blown it all on drugs and women! I continued writing Jilted John songs and performing gigs to get my Equity card. I also released *True Love Stories* which is now a cult album. But it was the work of a 19-year-old and I'm a bit embarrassed by songs like 'Fancy Mice'. After college, I went into repertory and did TV and radio. I'm John Shuttleworth now, of course, and I have several other stage characters including Brian Appleton, a failed rock star turned musicologist. I can't do Jilted John though. He was a teenager and I'm in my 40s. I'm waiting for someone to do a rap version. I'm just surprised nobody has sampled the guitar riff, because it's pretty good, isn't it?

'Perhaps I should have blown it all on drugs and women!'

TAMMY JONES

'Let Me Try Again' No 5, April 1975

TAMMY JONES: I began singing at an early age, and appeared on Welsh Radio and on TV in my own series *Tammy*. Eventually I went to England where I was introduced to Ernest Maxime, the head of the BBC. I auditioned for him, and after singing only a couple of lines, he booked me for a show called *Ice Cabaret*. That was my first big break. I began touring the clubs as a singer and my manager signed me to CBS. I had just finished with my boyfriend, and I wanted him to 'let me try again', so when I heard the song by Frank Sinatra, I started to sing it in my act. I sang the song when I went for an audition for *Opportunity Knocks*. It went down so well that the compere, Hughie Green, booked me for his show. I sang it a few times on TV before CBS decided to release it. Having promoted the song on *Opportunity Knocks*, Frank Sinatra's label decided to re-release his version on the strength of my publicity. I went up the charts and he didn't. My version was also helped into the charts by the fact that I sang a word wrong on the song, and the DJs wanted to hear where the mistake was – that meant a lot more plays. Crafty me, eh? I was driving to HTV studios when I heard on the radio that the record had gone into the charts at No 30. I nearly crashed the car. That evening I did a show in

Wales, where I was given champagne. Having a hit created a lot of opportunities for me. Unfortunately, at that time I had a manager who couldn't cope with the pressures of instant stardom and he messed things up. However, I did have lots of success from the record. I was careful with my money and immediately bought a house. I live in New Zealand now and am semi-retired. I still do shows, one of which is called 'Fish, Chips And Knees Up Mother Brown'. I have two albums out including *Easy Listening Country* and *The Answer to Everything*, which includes a new version of 'Let Me Try Again'. I think I sing it better these days!

'It was predicted that I would be a superstar.'

KURSAAL FLYERS

'Little Does She Know' No 14, November 1976
Line up: Paul Shuttleworth (vocals), Richie Bull (banjo), Will Birch (drums), Vic Collins (pedal steel), Graeme Douglas (lead guitar). Session orchestra produced by Mike Batt

PAUL SHUTTLEWORTH: The band comes from Southend-on-Sea where the Kursaal amusement park was a great landmark. Our music had a country rock flavour and so it seemed a perfect name for us. In the 60s, Will, Graeme and I were in a band called Surly Bird. Later I formed Cow Pie with Vic and Richie. In 1972, Will, Graeme, Vic, Richie, Dave Hatfield and myself got a gig at a local pub and we became the Kursaal Flyers. Our mates Dr Feelgood helped get us onto the London pub rock scene. We met Paul Conroy who became our manager and got us a deal with Jonathan King's UK Records. Later we signed to CBS and got together with Mike Batt, who produced *The Wombles*. Will and Graeme wrote 'Little Does She Know' for our album *Golden Mile*. Originally it was in waltz time, but we tried a Phil Spector-ish treatment. Mike really went to town. He hired most of the London Philharmonic to back my vocals and added choral singers, tubular bells and a shotgun. It was like the *1812 Overture*. Noel Edmonds played it on Radio 1 and I thought: 'We've cracked it now.' But while it was a Christmas hit, I can remember avoiding people collecting for charity because I didn't have any money. We'd spent loads on recording and that had to be repaid. But for a while it was magical. We wrote a follow-up single called 'Radio Romance' but the lyrics were a dig at Radio 1 and they refused to play it. I left the band to do some solo stuff with Mike Batt but Radio 1 still wouldn't play my records. Fortunately, I was a qualified graphic designer so I slipped back into that to pay the mortgage. Art and music are my two great loves and I've started painting again, so I'm quite happy. Will Birch has written a book called *No Sleep Till Canvey Island* which tells the story of pub rock. Two years ago I put together a new band with Graeme, and the Kursaals are flying again!

'**...tubular bells and a shotgun. It was like the *1812 Overture*.**'

LATIN QUARTER

'Radio Africa' No 14, September 1986

Line up: Mike Jones (lyrics), Steve Skaith (vocals, guitar), Richard Wright (guitar), Greg Harewood (bass), Richie Stevens (drums), Yona Dunsford (vocals, keyboards), Carol Douet (vocals), Steve Jeffries (keyboards)

DR MIKE JONES: I began writing songs when I was at Liverpool University. I don't sing and I don't play, but I can hear the songs in my head. I started collaborating with Steve Skaith, who I met in a far-left student organisation, and he put his melodies to my words. Steve then moved to London, and a friend promised he could get us a record deal. All the majors showed interest, but we weren't a band, and it took us a year to create a live line-up. However, we eventually signed to a new indie label, 'Rockin' Horse'. I wanted Latin Quarter to be a British version of Talking Heads, but as each song had its own approach, we tended to have a very eclectic, unfocused sound and identity. Nigel Gray, who produced the first Police album, produced our first single 'Radio Africa', which got to No 14 in the NME chart. We were pop stars! But it didn't last long. We played on the main stage at Glastonbury, sold out gigs in Germany, and in some European countries we stayed popular well into the 90s. However, with an eight-piece band and two managers the money didn't go far. We made an expensive third album, *Swimming Against The Stream*, in LA, only to return to the UK and find that House music had taken off, and nobody wanted our weird blend of politicised soft-core rock. Nevertheless, we carried on making albums, mostly for German indies.

During the 1990s I wrote a PhD thesis at Liverpool's Institute of Popular Music about our experiences. I'm now a Course Director of an MA in Music Industry Studies at the Institute. Steve Skaith lives in Mexico City and is still making records. Carol is a dietician and Yona is a successful session vocalist. Richard Wright is a classical session guitarist, Greg is with Go West, and Richie Stevens plays with Boy George. We had a great time with Latin Quarter. It was just frustrating that our success wasn't sustained and developed.

'We were pop stars! But it didn't last long.'

LOTUS EATERS

'The First Picture Of You' No 15, June 1983
Line up: Peter Coyle (vocals), Jeremy Kelly (guitars)

JEREMY KELLY: Peter and I began writing songs together in Liverpool in 1982. The first one was 'The First Picture Of You', which proved the right song at the right time. It was very melodic and acoustically orientated. When we turned up to do a Peel Session on Radio 1, John Peel was expecting Peter's other group the Jass Babies, instead, he ended up with the Lotus Eaters. After the broadcast, a bidding war ensued and we signed with Arista without having played a gig. At the time, acoustic bands such as ourselves, Orange Juice and Aztec Camera were very popular in Japan, where our music was termed Post Punk Neo Acoustic. 'The First Picture Of You' was the most played record in the UK in a week, and success happened incredibly quickly. It seemed obvious to us that the song would be a hit, as it sounded unique against 80s electro. Our belief in acoustic ambiance was justified when it got to No 15, but we couldn't celebrate because the bar at the YMCA, where we were staying to cut costs, was dry. After the hit, we toured Europe and released an album, but were later dropped by Arista.

Peter masterminded G-Love, a club in Liverpool, writing 'Sly One' for Marina Van Rooy, and song-smithing with The Lightning Seeds. He has released 8 solo albums and runs a men's mental health charity called Calm. I wrote with The Wild Swans and The Lovers, but then received an MA in theatre studies and became a freelance theatre director. In 2003 I devised and directed a multi-media play, *Missing*, staged at the Brighton Festival. Peter and I released a new album in 2001. The band is respected in Japan and the Philippines, and in August 2002 we performed a concert in Manila for 3,000 people. We are now working on a new album with strings, and reviving the true spirit of the Lotus Eaters.

'We couldn't celebrate because the bar was dry.'

RALPH McTELL

'Streets Of London' No 2, December 1974
Line up: *Ralph McTell (vocals, guitar, harmonica), Rod Clements (bass) and Prelude (vocal harmonies)*

RALPH McTELL: 'The Streets Of London' was written a long time before it was recorded. It wasn't about the homeless. It was inspired by a lonely friend who was a heroin addict. I was very young and naïve when I wrote the song and I couldn't write one like it now. I didn't want it on my first album *Eight Frames A Second* (1968). On my second album *Spiral Staircase* (1969), I wanted to mix blues and ragtime, and certainly didn't want an old song included, but producer Gus Dudgeon had heard 'Streets' and made it the album's first track. By 1974 my contract with Transatlantic had expired. They had steadfastly refused to put 'Streets' out as a single, believing it was 'too long and too sad'. My brother suggested I record it again, which I did. I gave it to Warner Brothers and after five years of promotion in the folk clubs, the song took off. In one day it sold 90,000 copies and was No 2 by Christmas. Even more extraordinary, there were three versions in the German charts – all by me! 'Streets' also sold more sheet music than any song since the war. Sadly, it was never a hit in America.

I formed a rock band just before the record was a hit, but of course we never played 'Streets'. Audiences didn't like the band, so I announced my retirement and went off to America in a fit of pique. I sat alone in a hotel with my guitar and wondered what the hell was going on. I was bewildered, depressed and confused. I came home, played a few dates and tried to put it all behind me. In truth 'Streets' opened more doors than it closed. The song is still played all over the world and even school children in the Himalayas have been heard singing it. I'm 58 now and have been on the road for 37 years. There have been lots of changes in my life and I'm blessed with fantastically loyal fans. I've lived the life of a travelling musician and it's been wonderful. I am taking time out from touring now, but I've still got a few ideas on the boil!

'...there were three versions of "Streets" in the German charts – all by me!'

MOCK TURTLES

'Can You Dig It?' No 18, March 1991
*Line up: Martin Coogan (vocals, guitar, composer), Martin Glyn Murray (guitar), Steve Cowen (drums), Andrew
Stewardson (bass) and Joanne Gent (keyboards)*

MARTIN COOGAN: Because we're a Manchester band, our first record company tried to lump us into the
'Madchester' scene. But we didn't go robbing cars or taking ecstasy. We were a good Indie band that could
knock out a tune. After contributing a track to a Syd Barrett tribute album, we were signed up to Imaginary
Records in 1987. 'Can You Dig It?' was a bit of an afterthought. We'd recorded 'Lay Me Down' and were due to
do a B side, but the sleeve info had to go off early. My manager said: 'What's the B side called?' I said: 'I haven't
written it yet.' He said: 'Just give me a title.' I said: 'Can You Dig It?' – there you go!' The following evening I had
friends round for dinner. I had to excuse myself to write the song in the back room, where I cobbled together
some lyrics and knocked out some chords. It took half an hour and then I went back to my meal. 'Lay Me Down'
got a lot of airplay but people preferred the B side. When we signed to Siren they wanted us to re-record 'Can
You Dig It?' and in March 1991 it was a Top 20 hit. But the follow-ups didn't sell as well. We did a ridiculously
expensive promo video in Venice and ran up a massive bill. Siren folded and we ended up on Virgin EMI, who
dropped us in 1993. It was tough and we suffered a rapid downward slide. Steve left and was replaced by
Smiley. We did our last gig four years ago. Then I got a message to call Virgin Music urgently. They said

Vodafone wanted to use 'Can You Dig It?' in a £25 million
advertising campaign, and as the songwriter, they needed my
permission. I said: 'Where do I sign?' Then Virgin Records wanted
to do a remix, so I called in Norman Cook, Mr Break Beat himself,
to do the job. The remix went back into the charts. In March 2003
we were back on *Top Of The Pops*. We've now done a new album
called *The Best Of* and have reformed for a tour.

'"Can You Dig It?" was a bit of
an afterthought.'

MONSOON

'Ever So Lonely' No 9, April 1982
Line up: Sheila Chandra (vocals), Martin Smith (bass), Steve Coe (keyboards, producer), Hugh Jones (producer)

SHEILA CHANDRA: I had been at the Italia Conti theatre school for five years before I had a hit record with Monsoon. I'd had a speaking part in *Grange Hill*, so it wasn't as though I'd been plucked off the streets. My voice had broken when I was 12 and this mature voice emerged. I knew then that I wanted to be a singer. I auditioned for a record company, which came to nothing. The tape lay around in a box for a couple of years, only to be discovered by composer Steve Coe, who was looking for a singer for his fusion project. Steve's neighbours had introduced him to Hindi film music with its gorgeous strings and he'd fallen in love with the sound. He needed a band to perform his material and this led to the idea of Monsoon. When he heard my voice he thought 'My God, that's the voice of Monsoon'. He got hold of my details, and when he found out I was Asian, he was convinced I would be perfect for the group. I was really excited about his song 'Ever So Lonely' because of the combination of Indian and Western cross rhythms. It was the first time a dedicated fusion band was in the charts with a dance-floor hit. During the instrumental section, people were dancing to an Indian classical raga, and I was immensely proud of that. I think everyone was surprised to see a 16-year-old Asian girl on *Top Of The Pops* wearing a sari.

Having released one album and four singles, Monsoon disbanded in November 1982 after disagreements with the record company. I went back to college to finish my A levels, then went solo. 'So Lonely' was a hit again for Jakatta in February 2002 when it got to No 8. They had baked the 20-year-old, two-inch magnetic tape for five days to make it playable. Then they reconstructed the track and used my original vocals, which was quite eerie – I like to be on *Top Of The Pops* once every 20 years, at least!

'People were dancing to an Indian classical raga.'

JOHN OTWAY

'Really Free' No 27, December 1977

Line up: John Otway (vocals), Wild Willy Barrett (guitar, fiddle)

JOHN OTWAY: When Wild Willy Barrett and myself appeared on BBC TV's *The Old Grey Whistle Test* in 1977, we became famous because of my leap onto Willy's amplifier: I split my legs and rolled around the floor in agony. My appearance was voted into the *Top Twenty Worst Moments on TV*. Although we were performing a different song, 'Really Free' was out and selling ten copies a day. The day after the show, the single started selling 5,000 a day and a week later it was in the charts. It was overnight stardom. At the next gig there was a queue round the block – they obviously expected me to do a leap every night! I thought it would be the start of a long chart career, which of course it was. I just didn't think it would take 25 years to get a follow-up. I had an odd kind of act with Willy. He was a bluegrass player and I couldn't really sing or play. I was just willing to do anything on stage – my first performance had been in the school playground, drinking a bottle of ink. The song became a catch phrase, and on some records it was called 'Cor Baby That's Really Free' but on the label it was just 'Really Free'. The obvious follow-up was the B side 'Beware Of The Flowers', but I brought out a ridiculous ballad instead, which was a flop.

Since then I've done a bit of acting and a few TV ads. In 2002 I celebrated my 50th birthday with a concert

at the London Palladium when I was back in the charts with 'Bunsen Burner', which got to No 9. It had taken me a quarter of a century to get back on *Top Of The Pops*. So now I'm a two hit wonder!

'My appearance was voted into the *Top Twenty Worst Moments on TV*.'

BRIAN PROTHEROE

'Pinball' No 22, September 1974

BRIAN PROTHEROE: I was an amateur musician and actor in my teens, growing up in Salisbury. I joined various bands and also worked as a lab technician. Later, I was in a group called Folk Blues Incorporated. I often met Paul Simon, when he was doing the London folk clubs. I then became a professional actor and toured in a thriller called *Death On Demand* in which I played a pop star. The writer of one of the songs I sang was very enthusiastic about my performance and encouraged me to send demos to a number of record companies. Chrysalis heard 'Pinball' and loved it. I'd written the song in 1972 when I was living with a neurotic cat in a flat in Covent Garden. I was out of work and had split up with my girlfriend. On one occasion I went to the pub and just played pinball. That day provided the inspiration for the song – a diary entry about feeling lonely. 'Pinball' was released as my first single and it felt extraordinary when it went into the charts. I remember Tony Coe played the jazz saxophone solo on the record. When we played 'Pinball' live he couldn't remember the session, let alone his solo. The funny thing was that after we did *Top Of The Pops* the song went *down* the charts. That wasn't supposed to happen. I never agreed with the record company's choice of follow-up singles and I felt uncomfortable with all the pop star hype. Nevertheless, I recorded three albums, which I'm proud of, and they have all been re-released on CD. I wrote some of the songs with Martin Duncan, who is now a director of Chichester Festival Theatre.

Nowadays, when I join a new acting company, someone always says 'Oh, I bought your hit'. I still write music but concentrate on acting, and in 2003 I was in a London production of Chekhov's *The Cherry Orchard*.

'After we did *Top Of The Pops* the song went *down* the charts.'

RENAISSANCE

'Northern Lights' No 10, July 1978
Line up: Annie Haslam (vocals), Michael Dunford (guitar), John Tout (keyboards), Jonathan Camp (bass, vocals), Terry Sullivan (drums)

MICHAEL DUNFORD: Surprised – that's how we felt when 'Northern Lights' was a hit in 1978. We were touring America when we heard the news. I had written the melody for the song and had then sent a cassette of the tune to Cornish poet Betty Thatcher, who wrote the lyrics about the Aurora Borealis. David Hentschell, who worked with Genesis and Elton John, produced the album and Annie's vocals were triple-tracked, which created a beautiful sound. After Dave Lee Travis made the single 'record of the week' on Radio 1, we appeared on *Top Of The Pops* three times. It was a real experience to have the BBC orchestra back us 'live', even though we were miming. Having a Top Ten hit was great fun, but we never saw any money. It was all wrapped up in record company advances. I suppose somebody had to pay for all that champagne!

We broke up around 1983, but revived Renaissance in 2000 for a new album called *Tuscany*. We also recorded a 'live' album in Japan but, sadly, couldn't afford to continue touring. Annie now lives in the States

where she has her own band and is getting into painting. I have a wonderful family and am involved in a West End theatre production of *Scheherazade*. Terry Sullivan has been working on a solo album and took part in our reunion in 2000. John Camp is no longer in touch, while John Tout worked as a Telex operator after leaving Renaissance.

'Surprised – that's how we felt when "Northern Lights" was a hit.'

ROMAN HOLLIDAY

'Don't Try To Stop It' No 14, July 1983

Line up: *Steve Lambert (vocals), Brian Bonhomme (guitar, vocals), Adrian York (keyboards), Jon Durno (bass), Simon Cohen (drums), Rob Lambert (sax), John Eacott (trumpet)*

BRIAN BONHOMME: I had been in a number of local bands in Harlow, Essex, where I was born, before I formed Roman Holliday. I put an ad in the local paper and several of the people who answered became members of the band. We kicked around a bunch of different musical styles until we hit on the swing/jive thing. Everyone had different musical tastes, so it was a volatile mix, but it worked for a while. We got a record deal largely thanks to John Peel, who saw us at a club called the Jive Dive in London's Soho and offered us a session on his radio show. That's what got us noticed by Jive Records. We were really excited when our second single 'Don't Try To Stop It' got to No 14, and we didn't think we would end up as one hit wonders. We hoped our success would last a bit longer, but it didn't. Nonetheless, we soon found ourselves travelling to Europe, America and Japan, and a US tour with the Stray Cats was probably the highlight. Unfortunately, we didn't make much money from the hit. To be honest, we could probably have done better financially working in a warehouse shifting boxes – though being in the band was a lot more interesting, obviously! In 1985, the band broke up. Subsequently, I got

out of the music business, moved to New York, and went to university to study history. I eventually got a doctoral degree and now teach at a university in Arkansas. Roman Holliday got together again for a one-off reunion gig

at the Borderline in London in July 2001, which was a lot of fun. I still dabble in music and have self-released two solo albums, *World Keeps Turning* (2001) and *The River And The Mill* (2002). Jon went on to be Musical Director for page 3 girl Sam Fox. He now runs a small engineering firm. Simon is a London cab driver by day and percussionist by night. He has also written a really cool Christmas song called 'Yippee Christmas', which he is looking to release.

'We got a record deal largely thanks to John Peel.'

SPLODGENESSABOUNDS

'Two Pints Of Lager And A Packet Of Crisps Please' No 7, June 1980
Line up: Max Splodge (vocals, guitar), Roger Rodent (bass) and Desert Island Joe (drums)

MAX SPLODGE: In 1979 a whole bunch of us musicians were living in a squat in Chislehurst. We entered the Melody Maker Rock Folk contest as a 13-piece band called Splodgenessabounds. I was lead vocalist, the bass player was on synthesizer… it was just a total shambles. In the contest we came on tap dancing, stark naked with cardboard boxes on our heads. We did three songs, none longer than a minute and got *nil points* for musical ability but ten points for originality. We came third and won £200 and an amplifier. Afterwards a guy from Decca asked if we wanted to make a record. I said 'no thanks'. But he followed us to the pub and promised us a £1,000 cash advance. We recorded an A side called 'Simon Templar'. One night I rushed into The Crown in Chislehurst waving a pound note, trying to buy two pints of lager and a packet of crisps. The bell rang and the bloke wouldn't serve me. The guys in the band were out of their heads on magic mushrooms and thought this was hysterical. The next day I put down a drum track and bass line and just shouted, 'two pints of lager and a packet of crisps please…' Mike Reid played it on Radio 1 and it started selling 17,000 copies a day. No one could believe it. It sold a quarter of a million copies and got to No 7. The publishing rights are a sore point. They were sold when the publishers went bust. I only got £240. But in 2002 the song was used as an advert in Scandinavia and I got

some money at last. Splodgenessabounds stills tours. Over the last 20 years there have been seven deaths of people who have been in the band at one time, mainly from heart attacks and liver failures, including Roger Rodent who died in 2002. Miles Runt Flat who played guitar in the first line up is now the stage manager of the Astoria in London. Winston Forbes (keyboards) and Pat Thetic (guitar) are electricians and Whiffy Archer who played paper and comb runs a naked Bungee jumping firm. Baby Greensleeves, our first vocalist, is a bingo caller in Thames Ditton.

'We came on tap dancing, naked…'

TWINKLE

'Terry' No 4, November 1964

TWINKLE (LYNN ANNETTE RIPLEY): I wrote 'Terry', which was about a biker, when I was 14. I used to sing with a band of schoolboys called The Trekkers. I'd do two numbers on a Saturday night, one of which was 'Terry'. I had no problem getting the song published because my sister, Dawn James, was a pop journalist on *Mirabelle* magazine and knew everyone in the business. When 'Terry' made the charts I was having dinner with Clodagh Rogers. My manager Phil Solomon rang and said 'You're in the charts'. I returned to the table and sat down. Clodagh said: 'My God, if somebody told me I was in the charts, I wouldn't just sit there eating my dinner.' But, because I had bags of confidence, I would have been shocked if it *hadn't* been a hit. However, I was never a prima donna; I just wasn't nervous. And, although I was only 16, I pretended to be a year older.

'Terry' got to No 3 in the NME and we did *Top Of The Pops* at a studio in a church hall in Manchester. Thankfully the church burned down so all the video footage of me was lost. There's only one clip from the 1965 NME Poll Winners concert, where I look and sound like nothing on earth. My first 'live' gig was with Jerry Lee Lewis and the second with the Rolling Stones. I toured Ireland with the Stones and that was hysterical. I used

to go to all the parties and went out with Herman for a while. I loved Rod Stewart, too. I often think of asking him, 'When are you gonna give me some money, now you're rolling in it me old mate?' When I went to France on holiday and nobody recognised me, I realised that I didn't need the pop business anymore. I've been married for 30 years, and we've got two children and loads of dogs, cats and chickens. It's just lots of mouths waiting to be fed – I hope someone covers 'Terry' soon! I did sing on the 60s nostalgia circuit a few years ago; and I toured with The Four Pennies and did a show with Cynthia Lennon. I'm still writing songs, but I don't think about the 60s unless somebody asks me.

'My first "live" gig was with Jerry Lee Lewis.'

TYPICALLY TROPICAL

'Barbados' No 1, August 1975
Line up: Jeff Calvert (vocals, guitar), Max West (real name Geraint Hughes) (vocals, guitar)

GERAINT HUGHES: I was born in Yorkshire in 1953, but my parents were from Port Talbot. We moved to London, where I studied classical guitar as a child. Later, I formed a small band. Jeff Calvert lived in the same street and often listened to us play. His dad was the director of Morgan studios which came in handy when we started writing songs together. We recorded them at night, sneaking behind the studios' doorman's back. One day Jeff thought of this reggae idea. He came up with a 'hook' and we put 'Typically Tropical' together during an afternoon at my parents' house. We snuck in to the studios, recorded a demo and gave it to Monty Babson, a director of Morgan. We were given a budget and recorded the song with hot session men like Chris Spedding. He wasn't too impressed with the chords we'd come up with but that didn't matter because he played guitar brilliantly. I then changed my name. People had always had trouble pronouncing Geraint so I used the pen name Max West, which caused a lot of confusion.

I was on holiday in Portugal when Jeff rang to say that 'Barbados' was in the charts. It was an agonising climb before it got to No 1. We weren't hailed as reggae stars. We were two rather boring-looking, white recording engineers! But we got a special *Music Week* award for being No 1 with our first release. We knew we were one hit wonders – 'Barbados' was a one-off fluke. But when it was covered in 1999 by The Venga Boys as 'We're Going To Ibiza', it went to No 1 again. Today, I do experimental TV stuff and library music. Jeff has his own recording studio in his garden. After the hit he learned to fly; and in true Barbados Coconut Airways spirit he is now an accomplished pilot!

'"Barbados" was a one-off fluke.'

JUDIE TZUKE

'Stay With Me Till Dawn' No 16, July 1979

JUDIE TZUKE: My dad was Sefton Myers, a theatrical 'angel' who supported Andrew Lloyd Webber and Tim Rice when they wrote *Jesus Christ Superstar*. As a young girl, I remember coming home from school to find Andrew playing piano upstairs in my dad's flat. Peter Sellers lived on the other side of the hall. I began playing guitar and writing songs as a teenager. Tim and Andrew wanted to record my first song 'Revolution', but it was pretty dire! Dad died when I was 14 and this greatly affected me. I went off on all sorts of tangents, and it was five years before I did my first album *Welcome To The Cruise*. A boyfriend had said to me: 'If you get famous, I won't want to go out with you.' So I stopped trying to be successful, until I realised he was an idiot. 'Stay With Me Till Dawn' and my first single 'For You' were written on the same night when I was 18. People thought 'Stay With Me' was quite rude and suggestive. I really didn't see it like that. It was actually about a good male friend of mine and how we comforted each other when we split up with boyfriends. My musical partner, Mike Paxman,

had written a disco track called 'Need You Tonight' and he came over and sang me a bit which went with my verse. We slowed it down, put it together and the whole thing made sense. We knew it was going to be special. I woke my mum up at 5 a.m. and played it to her. 'Stay With Me' was released on Elton John's Rocket label. When it was a hit, I went on tour supporting Elton. He was on a first class jet – we were on a bus! When I was famous, I felt quite uncomfortable. I loved singing and writing songs but hated being looked at. I was known as a ballad singer but I was quite 'rocky' really. Right now I'm doing so much stuff. I have my own record label and sell my albums through the internet. I work with a lot of 'chill out' artists, and I'm also recording a new album of favourite songs including 'Hey Jude'.

'People thought "Stay With Me" was quite rude and suggestive.'

FRED WEDLOCK

'The Oldest Swinger In Town' No 6, February 1981
Line up: Fred Wedlock (vocals, guitar), Chris Newman (guitar)

FRED WEDLOCK: I never ever felt like I was the oldest swinger in town. And I wasn't guilty of being fashionable or energetic on a dance floor. But I was once spotted wearing crushed velvet loons. I started out playing banjo at college in the 60s. A mate introduced me to American folk music and it was such a revelation that I became a folk singer. I gradually moved in the direction of comedy which I found a useful device for getting free beer. After college I worked as a teacher. It was ages before I became a professional singer. I sang mainly in folk clubs in Bristol before I chanced my arm in London. I discovered the original version of 'The Oldest Swinger In Town', which was written by Ed Pickford, and I rewrote it substantially. Chris Newman arranged it for an LP on our own label. My manager, Kevin Wyatt-Lown, told me I should release it as a single. Kevin cut a 1,000 copies and in 1980, DJ Noel Edmonds played the song twice during the same Sunday morning show. He said: 'This is fantastic, it's gonna be a hit.' Then the phone started ringing and it didn't stop for months. Everything went mad because we weren't signed. EMI rejected 'Swinger' because they didn't see the potential, but it might have been because the song was too descriptive of people in the record industry. Eventually we signed to Elton John's Rocket label and it got to No 6. I think it reached No 1 in Zimbabwe! These days every disco plays the song

and it still gets dragged out for 50th birthday parties and 25th wedding anniversaries. Lines like 'It takes all night to do what you used to do all night' always go down well. The money wasn't fabulous, but the hit opened a lot of doors. I've been a TV presenter for over 35 years doing shows like *Bargain Hunters* for HTV, and I've been able to perform all over the world. Despite having a heart attack a few years ago, I'm not planning on retiring. I will only retire when people stop ringing up and booking me!

'Noel Edmonds said: "This is fantastic, it's going to be a hit."'

WHITE TOWN

'Your Woman' No 1, January 1997
Jyoti Mishra (vocals, guitar, sequencer and samples)

JYOTI MISHRA: I started playing keyboards when I was 12. I became a one-man synth band, learned the guitar and formed White Town in 1989. The rest of the band started leaving and I was on my own again. I recorded 'Your Woman' in my home studio in Derby. There's nobody else on the record except me. It was done with a second-hand sequencer, sampler and me singing and playing guitar. The sample was from a 1932 song sung by Al Bowlly and played by Lew Stone. It was inspired by the BBC TV series *Pennies From Heaven* by Dennis Potter. 'Your Woman' first came out on the American Indie label Parasol in July 1996. I'd been a DJ since 1987 and started playing the record to test it out. The reaction was amazing. My girlfriend suggested I send it off somewhere. But I'm not exactly the easiest package to sell: some fat Asian bloke who does his own recordings? It's not going to challenge Kylie, is it?! I didn't have much money and could only afford to send off five copies. Three went to DJs including Mark Radcliffe and Simon Mayo, who played it on Radio 1. I became the most requested record on the show. I even made the papers: 'Bloke in bedroom makes record.' I had more requests than Oasis and was quite

freaked out. Woolworths wanted 10,000 copies. But my American label only wanted to do 500. They didn't understand how important national radio is in the UK. When I said they needed to press 20,000 they thought I was getting over excited. Then I was signed to EMI in December 1996 and the record came out in 1997. It was No 1 in Britain and eight other countries. I knew I would be a one hit wonder. People were very strange towards me when I had a hit. Musicians who consistently said my stuff was rubbish suddenly changed their tune. And I became a lot more attractive to women. Amazing! I couldn't leave my house because people would start whistling my song at me, which became a bit wearing. If I had the chance to have a hit single again I'd probably say 'no'… unless they offered me twenty million quid.

'Bloke in bedroom makes record.'

PETE WINGFIELD

'Eighteen With A Bullet' No 7, June 1975

PETE WINGFIELD: I had my own blues band Jellybread in the late 60s, then played keyboards with the Keef Hartley Band, Colin Blunstone, and Maggie Bell. I signed with Island Records as a solo artist in 1975, and the song was on my album *Breakfast Special*. I was always an avid soul record collector who loved poring over the Billboard charts, and the song was a tongue-in-cheek combination of doo-wop love song and record-biz jargon. In writing it I'd had the Dells vocal group in mind, imagining the guttural lead of Marvin Junior, the falsetto of Johnny Carter, and the bass of Chuck Barksdale – but I ended up doing all the voices myself. In the States it was a big R&B hit long before it crossed over pop to reach No 5 on the Billboard charts in October 1975. One week the record was actually *at* 18 with a bullet in all three US trade papers. When it came to the album, though, I fell victim to my own youthful stupidity. Island in the US didn't want to use the UK sleeve with my picture on it, as it was to be marketed as an R&B album, and black Americans were reluctant to buy records by white artists at the time. I insisted on using it, and sure enough, the album didn't sell in the US. I'm still proud of the

song, which was used recently in the soundtrack of the movie *Lock, Stock and Two Smoking Barrels*. I'm even in the Rock'n'Roll Hall of Fame in Cleveland, on the Wall of One Hit Wonders – which wouldn't be so if I'd had another hit! I carried on doing sessions and working for other people during and after that period – in fact, I was on the road with the Hollies in Australia while the record was in the UK chart. Since then I've spent 18 years with the Everly Brothers' band, as well as playing on hundreds of records and chalking up a few hits as a producer. In 1999 I played on Paul McCartney's *Run Devil Run* album. You can see me in the 'At the Cavern' video, my white hair glistening behind him. I used to be salt 'n' pepper – now I'm just salt!

'The song was on the soundtrack of *Lock, Stock and Two Smoking Barrels.***'**

TRACIE YOUNG

'The House That Jack Built' No 9, March 1983

TRACIE YOUNG: I'd always wanted to be a singer and one day I came across an advert in *Smash Hits* placed by Paul Weller, looking for young artists to sign to his record label. He wanted someone aged between 18 and 22. I taped myself singing into the home stereo and sent the cassette off. A few days later mum got a phone call. It was Jill, Paul's girlfriend. Could I go for an audition? I was flabbergasted. I met Paul and sang for him. We talked about tastes in music and he gave me a demo of 'The House That Jack Built' by The Questions to learn. Meanwhile, I provided backing vocals on the Jam's last single 'Beat Surrender', which was No 1 in December 1982. I was also on the first Style Council single 'Speak Like A Child'. When I went on *Top Of The Pops* with 'The House That Jack Built' I'd just turned 18 and was famous overnight. But it all disappeared just as quickly. I couldn't sing 'live' in the same way as I sounded on the record, because my voice had been speeded up. I sounded like Minnie Mouse on helium. Then we had a major falling out about the next record. I was being obstinate and difficult, and Paul wouldn't compromise. We had a blazing row because I hated the song. Then, in 1985, I recorded a song I loved called 'I Can't Leave You Alone' that never got higher than No 60. I was

devastated. Soon after that I stopped singing and put the music business behind me.

In 1989 I got married and moved to the Midlands where I ran a couple of pubs for eight years. Then we moved to Southend and I joined Essex FM doing the traffic and travel reports. I've now got my own *Tracie Young Show* on Sunday afternoons. But I never play my old records because I don't like them! In February 2003 I appeared in the line up on *Never Mind The Buzzcocks*. It was scary but the memories came flooding back.

'I was famous overnight. But it all disappeared just as quickly.'

ZOMBIES

'She's Not There' No 12, September 1964
Line up: *Rod Argent (piano), Colin Blunstone (vocals), Paul Atkinson (guitar), Chris White (bass), Hugh Grundy (drums)*

ROD ARGENT: We formed the Zombies in 1962 and built up a local following. We were just leaving school when our group entered and won the 'Herts Beat' contest in Watford in 1964. The prize was a Decca recording contract. I was over the moon and everyone wanted to turn professional, although Paul Atkinson's parents wanted him to go to university. Our first single was going to be Gershwin's 'Summertime', but producer Ken Jones said: 'You should write something yourselves.' I was full of naïve confidence and wrote 'She's Not There', which had a minor to major chord sequence. Chris White wrote 'You Make Me Feel Good' and it was a toss-up which would be the A side. In the end 'She's Not There' was released. George Harrison saw us on *Juke Box Jury* and loved the song. After that programme the single went on to tickle the UK Top 10. However, it reached No 2 in America and No 1 in Japan and Australia. We had lots more hits, but not in England. We were lucky to have such a big success with our first single, which Colin sang beautifully. Sadly, we couldn't get another UK chart-topper and this caused us to break up in 1967. But, by then we had recorded the album *Odessey And Oracle* which spawned 'Time Of The Season', our biggest US hit. In the 70s I formed my group Argent, and Colin had a successful solo career. Hugh Grundy went to work for CBS and later ran a pub. Paul Atkinson went to America and became vice president of RCA. I worked as a producer and session man, but am touring and recording again with Colin, and having a ball. The original Zombies held a reunion in 1997 at the Jazz Café in London where we played 'She's Not There' for the first time in 30 years, and it went down a storm.

'George Harrison saw us on *Juke Box Jury* and loved the song.'

ONE HIT WONDERS OF THE 1960s

This is by no means a fully comprehensive list of one hit wonders of the last 40 years. What is offered here are some of the best-known and best-loved British artists whose smash hits helped define the sound of pop.

The 60s was a decade of frantic activity, when young people took over the music industry. Record companies allied to Tin Pan Alley tunesmiths had made hits to order. All that changed with the Beatles, when Lennon and McCartney showed artists could write their own songs. The 60s began with Elvis and Cliff and ended with Jimi Hendrix and the Bee Gees. It was a high old time.

ARTIST	HIT TITLE	CHART POSITION	YEAR
MICHAEL COX	Angela Jones	7	1960
MAX HARRIS	Gurney Slade	11	1960
BRYAN JOHNSON	Looking High, High, High	20	1960
RICKY VALANCE	Tell Laura I Love Her	1	1960
CLEO LAINE	You'll Answer To Me	5	1961
MRS MILLS	Mrs Mills Medley	18	1961
LOUISE CORDET	I'm Just A Baby	13	1962
JOHNNY KEATING	Theme From 'Z Cars'	8	1962
SUSAN MAUGHAN	Bobby's Girl	3	1962
DORA BRYAN	All I Want For Christmas Is A Beatle	20	1963
CARAVELLES	You Don't Have To Be A Baby To Cry	6	1963
CHRIS SANDFORD	Not Too Little – Not Too Much	17	1963
TWINKLE	Terry	4	1964
ZOMBIES	She's Not There	12	1964
HEDGEHOPPERS ANONYMOUS	It's Good News Week	5	1965
SORROW	Take A Heart	21	1965
JACKIE TRENT	Where Are You Now?	1	1965

GRAHAM BONNEY	Supergirl	19	1966
NEIL CHRISTIAN	That's Nice	14	1966
MERSEYS	Sorrow	4	1966
OVERLANDERS	Michelle	1	1966
PINKERTON'S ASSORTED COLOURS	Mirror Mirror	9	1966
SIMON DUPREE AND THE BIG SOUND	Kites	9	1967
FRANKIE MCBRIDE	Five Little Fingers	19	1967
KEITH WEST	Excerpt From A Teenage Opera	2	1967
BEDROCKS	Ob-La-Di, Ob-La-Da	20	1968
BONZO DOG DOO-DAH BAND	I'm The Urban Spaceman	5	1968
CRAZY WORLD OF ARTHUR BROWN	Fire	1	1968
JULIE DRISCOLL, BRIAN AUGER AND THE TRINITY	This Wheel's On Fire	5	1968
GUN	Race With The Devil	8	1968
HONEYBUS	I Can't Let Maggie Go	8	1968
LOVE SCULPTURE	Sabre Dance	5	1968
SUE NICHOLLS	Where Will You Be?	17	1968
PAPER DOLLS	Something Here In My Heart Keeps Tellin' Me No	11	1968
PLASTIC PENNY	Everything I Am	6	1968
FAMILY DOGG	A Way Of Life	6	1969
NOEL HARRISON	The Windmills Of Your Mind	8	1969
HUMBLE PIE	Natural Born Bugie	4	1969
THUNDERCLAP NEWMAN	Something In The Air	1	1969
KAREN YOUNG	Nobody's Child	6	1969

ONE HIT WONDERS OF THE 1970s

Glam rock, reggae and soul dominated the hyperactive 70s, unleashing new pop idols such as Marc Bolan, Bob Marley and Barry White. The decade began with classic No 1 smash 'Spirit In The Sky' by Norman Greenbaum. It later saw Paul McCartney launch his Wings, while folk singer Ralph McTell took his fans around 'The Streets Of London' – until the Sex Pistols ruled, okay.

ARTIST	HIT TITLE	CHART POSITION	YEAR
BUTTERSCOTCH	Don't You Know	17	1970
EDISON LIGHTHOUSE	Love Grows (Where My Rosemary Goes)	1	1970
HOTLEGS	Neanderthal Man	2	1970
JUICY LUCY	Who Do You Love?	14	1970
MATTHEWS SOUTHERN COMFORT	Woodstock	1	1970
MR BLOE	Groovin' With Mr Bloe	2	1970
CONGREGATION	Softly Whispering I Love You	4	1971
CURVED AIR	Back Street Luv	4	1971
EAST OF EDEN	Jig A Jig	7	1971
JOHNNY PEARSON	Sleepy Shores	8	1971
PIGLETS	Johnny Reggae	3	1971
SPRINGWATER	I Will Return	5	1971
HARLEY QUINNE	New Orleans	19	1972
MARDI GRAS	Too Busy Thinking 'Bout My Baby	19	1972
GUY DARRELL	I've Been Hurt	12	1973
STUART GILLIES	Amanda	13	1973
HOTSHOTS	Snoopy Vs The Red Baron	4	1973
CLIFFORD T WARD	Gaye	8	1973

MICHAEL WARD	Let There Be Peace On Earth	⑮	1973
JOHN ASHER	Let's Twist Again	⑭	1974
FIRST CLASS	Beach Baby	⑬	1974
WAYNE GIBSON	Under My Thumb	⑰	1974
RALPH McTELL	Streets Of London	❷	1974
BRIAN PROTHEROE	Pinball	㉒	1974
SPLINTER	Costafine Town	⑰	1974
SUNNY	Doctor's Orders	❼	1974
MIKE BATT WITH THE NEW EDITION	Summertime City	❹	1975
GARY BENSON	Don't Throw It All Away	⑳	1975
JASPER CARROTT	Funky Moped/Magic Roundabout	❺	1975
BILLY HOWARD	King Of The Cops	❻	1975
JIGSAW	Sky High	❾	1975
TAMMY JONES	Let Me Try Again	❺	1975
TYPICALLY TROPICAL	Barbados	❶	1975
PETE WINGFIELD	Eighteen With A Bullet	❼	1975
CLIMAX BLUES BAND	Couldn't Get It Right	⑩	1976
KURSAAL FLYERS	Little Does She Know	⑭	1976
LAURIE LINGO AND THE DIPSTICKS	Convoy GB	❹	1976
M AND O BAND	Let's Do The Latin Hustle	⑯	1976
OUR KID	You Just Might See Me Cry	❷	1976
ROBIN SARSTEDT	My Resistance Is Low	❸	1976
THE ADVERTS	Gary Gilmore's Eyes	⑱	1977
BLUE	Gonna Capture Your Heart	⑱	1977
BRENDON	Gimme Some	⑭	1977
BRIGHOUSE AND RASTRICK BRASS BAND	The Floral Dance	❷	1977

BROTHERS	Sing Me	8	1977
DEAD END KIDS	Have I The Right?	6	1977
EDDIE AND THE HOT RODS	Do Anything You Wanna Do	9	1977
BERNI FLINT	I Don't Want To Put A Hold On You	3	1977
STEVE GIBBONS BAND	Tulane	12	1977
JOHN OTWAY	Really Free	27	1977
DAVID PARTON	Isn't She Lovely?	4	1977
RACING CARS	They Shoot Horses Don't They?	14	1977
BRIAN AND MICHAEL	Matchstalk Men and Matchstalk Cats and Dogs	1	1978
ANDY CAMERON	Ally's Tartan Army	6	1978
DRIVER 67	Car 67	7	1978
SCOTT FITZGERALD	If I Had Words	3	1978
JAMES GALWAY	Annie's Song	3	1978
GOLDIE	Making Up Again	7	1978
DEE D JACKSON	Automatic Lover	4	1978
MICK JACKSON	Blame It On the Boogie	15	1978
JILTED JOHN	Jilted John	4	1978
RICHARD MYHILL	It Takes Two To Tango	17	1978
SALLY OLDFIELD	Mirrors	19	1978
RENAISSANCE	Northern Lights	10	1978
TONIGHT	Drummer Man	14	1978
FIDDLER'S DRAM	Day Trip To Bangor	4	1979
FLYING LIZARDS	Money (That's What I Want)	4	1979
BILL LOVELADY	Reggae For It Now	12	1979
LENA MARTELL	One Day At A Time	1	1979
QUANTUM JUMP	The Lone Ranger	5	1979
RAMBLERS	The Sparrow	11	1979
JUDIE TZUKE	Stay With Me Till Dawn	16	1979
IRIS WILLIAMS	He Was Beautiful	18	1979

ONE HIT WONDERS OF THE 1980s

Digital recording, synthesizers and drum machines impacted on exciting new groups like Frankie Goes To Hollywood, while rap and metal toughed it out on the streets. Phil Collins was 'In The Air Tonight' and the Police and Genesis traded chart places with Adam & The Ants, Wham!, Michael Jackson, Madonna and Suggs. It was all Madness.

ARTIST	HIT TITLE	CHART POSITION	YEAR
AIR SUPPLY	All Out of Love	11	1980
LOOK	I Am The Beat	6	1980
ST WINIFRED'S SCHOOL CHOIR	There's No One Quite Like Grandma	1	1980
SPLODGENESSABOUNDS	Two Pints Of Lager And A Packet Of Crisps Please	7	1980
ANEKA	Japanese Boy	1	1981
GRAHAM BONNET	Night Games	6	1981
BROWN SAUCE	I Wanna Be A Winner	15	1981
TONY CAPSTICK AND THE CARLTON MAIN	The Sheffield Grinder/ Capstick Comes Home	3	1981
EVASIONS	Wikka Wrap	20	1981
SUSAN FASSBENDER	Twilight Cafe	21	1981
KEITH MARSHALL	Only Crying	12	1981
KATE ROBBINS AND BEYOND	More Than In Love	2	1981
STARTRAX	Startrax Club Disco	18	1981
FRED WEDLOCK	Oldest Swinger In Town	6	1981
BARDO	One Step Further	2	1982
BLUE ZOO	Cry Boy Cry	13	1982
THE BRAT	Chalk Dust: The Umpire Strikes Back	19	1982

KEITH HARRIS AND ORVILLE	Orville's Song	❹	1982
INCANTATION	Cacharpaya	⓬	1982
MAISONETTES	Heartache Avenue	❼	1982
MOBILES	Drowning in Berlin	❾	1982
MONSOON	Ever So Lonely	❾	1982
NATASHA	Iko Iko	❿	1982
PINKEES	Danger Games	❽	1982
FUNK MASTERS	It's Over	❽	1983
H 20	Dream To Sleep	⓱	1983
JIMMY THE HOOVER	Tantalise	⓲	1983
KISSING THE PINK	Last Film	⓳	1983
LOTUS EATERS	The First Picture Of You	⓯	1983
ROMAN HOLLIDAY	Don't Try To Stop It	⓮	1983
TRACIE YOUNG	The House That Jack Built	❾	1983
BELLE AND THE DEVOTIONS	Love Games	⓫	1984
SMILEY CULTURE	Police Officer	⓬	1984
JOE FAGIN	That's Livin' Alright	❸	1984
FICTION FACTORY	(Feels Like) Heaven	❻	1984
MURRAY HEAD	One Night In Bangkok	⓬	1984
NEIL	Hole In My Shoe	❷	1984
JOHN WAITE	Missing You	❾	1984
BIG SOUND AUTHORITY	This House (Is Where Your Love Stands)	㉑	1985
COMMENTATORS	N-N-Nineteen Not Out	⓭	1985
DREAM ACADEMY	Life In A Northern Town	⓯	1985
ALED JONES	Walking In The Air	❺	1985
CLAIRE AND FRIENDS	It's 'Orrible Being In Love	⓭	1986
LETITIA DEAN AND PAUL MEDFORD	Something Outa Nothing	⓬	1986

ANITA DOBSON	Anyone Can Fall In Love	4	1986
DOCTOR AND THE MEDICS	Spirit In The Sky	1	1986
FURNITURE	Brilliant Mind	21	1986
GRANGE HILL CAST	Just Say No	5	1986
HAYWOODE	Roses	11	1986
HOLLYWOOD BEYOND	What's The Colour Of Money?	7	1986
IT'S IMMATERIAL	Driving Away From Home (Jim's Tune)	18	1986
LATIN QUARTER	Radio Africa	14	1986
OWEN PAUL	My Favourite Waste Of Time	3	1986
BOOGIE BOX HIGH	Jive Talkin'	7	1987
BROKEN ENGLISH	Comin' On Strong	18	1987
MICHAEL CRAWFORD	The Music Of The Night	7	1987
KAREL FIALKA	Hey Matthew	9	1987
GLEN AND CHRIS	Diamond Lights	12	1987
KRUSH	House Arrest	3	1987
M/A/R/R/S	Pump Up The Volume	1	1987
MORRIS MINOR AND THE MAJORS	Stutter Rap	4	1987
TAFFY	I Love My Radio	6	1987
BREATHE	Hands To Heaven	4	1988
HARRY ENFIELD	Loadsamoney	4	1988
FUNKY WORM	Hustle!	13	1988
JACK 'N' CHILL	The Jack That House Built	6	1988
LYNNE HAMILTON	On The Inside	3	1989
HALO JAMES	Could Have Told You So	6	1989
REYNOLDS GIRLS	I'd Rather Jack	8	1989

ONE HIT WONDERS OF THE 1990s

Astonishing diversity, fragmentation of styles and 'in your face' youth culture typified the aggressive 90s. It was also a decade dominated by divas like Kylie Minogue and Sinead O'Connor, while boy band Take That fended off U2, Queen and Nirvana. Oasis, Blur and the Brit Pop phenomenon brought back the spirit of the 60s. Our one hit wonders were ready to take them all on – and win!

GROUP NAME	SONG NAME,	CHART POSITION	YEAR
CANDY FLIP	Strawberry Fields Forever	3	1990
E-ZEE POSSEE	Everything Starts With An 'E'	15	1990
FAB	Thunderbirds Are Go	5	1990
CHAD JACKSON	Hear The Drummer (Get Wicked)	3	1990
LFO	LFO	12	1990
PATRICK MACNEE AND HONOR BLACKMAN	Kinky Boots	5	1990
TOGETHER	Hardcore Uproar	12	1990
ARNEE AND THE TERMINATORS	I'll Be Back	5	1991
BANDERAS	This Is Your Life	16	1991
COLA BOY	7 Ways To Love	8	1991
CONTROL	Dance With Me	17	1991
HALE AND PACE AND THE STONKERS	The Stonk	1	1991
THE MOCK TURTLES	Can You Dig it?	18	1991
PRAISE	Only You	4	1991
DR SPIN	Tetris	6	1992
DON-E	Love Makes The World Go Round	18	1992
KICKS LIKE A MULE	The Bouncer	7	1992

SLIPSTREEM	We Are Raving – The Anthem	⑱	1992
SMART E'S	Sesame's Treet	②	1992
CAT	Tongue Tied	⑰	1993
LESLEY GARRETT AND AMANDA THOMPSON	Ave Maria	⑯	1993
WEST END	The Love I Lost	③	1993
T-EMPO	Saturday Night Sunday Morning	⑲	1994
TINMAN	Eighteen Strings	⑨	1994
ROY 'CHUBBY' BROWN	Living Next Door To Alice	③	1995
LOVE CITY GROOVE	Love City Groove	⑦	1995
PERFECTO ALLSTARZ	Reach Up	⑥	1995
DARREN DAY	Summer Holiday Medley	⑰	1996
KEN DOH	Nagasaki EP	⑦	1996
DUNBLANE	Knockin' On Heaven's Door/ Throw These Guns Away	①	1996
GOLDBUG	Whole Lotta Love	③	1996
ME ME ME	Hanging Around	⑲	1996
CHICKEN SHED THEATRE	I Am In Love With The World	⑮	1997
WHITE TOWN	Your Woman	①	1997
CAST FROM CASUALTY	Everlasting Love	⑤	1998
DENISE AND JOHNNY	Especially For You	③	1998
JANE MCDONALD	Cruise Into Christmas Medley	⑩	1998
PERPETUAL MOTION	Keep On Dancin'	⑫	1998
TOUCH & GO	Would You...?	③	1998
EMMIE	More Than This	⑤	1999
ENGLAND UNITED	(How Does It Feel To Be) On Top Of The World	⑨	1998
PETE HELLER	Big Love	⑫	1999

First published in 2003 by
New Holland Publishers (UK) Ltd
London • Cape Town • Sydney • Auckland
www.newhollandpublishers.com

Garfield House
86-88 Edgware Road
London W2 2EA
United Kingdom

80 McKenzie Street
Cape Town 8001
South Africa

Level 1, Unit 4
Suite 411, 14 Aquatic Drive
Frenchs Forest, NSW 2086
Australia

218 Lake Road
Northcote
Auckland
New Zealand

10 9 8 7 6 5 4 3 2 1

Publishing Manager: Jo Hemmings
Project Editor: Camilla MacWhannell
Designer: Alan Marshall
Production: Joan Woodroffe

Reproduction by Modern Age Repro House Ltd, Hong Kong
Printed and bound by Craft Print International Pte Ltd,
Singapore.

ISBN 1 84330 496 1